3⁹⁵

To Helen
sincerely,
Zelda M. Peters

Memory,

God's Golden
Window

Thanks for the m...

D1160550

Memory,

God's Golden Window

By Zelda M. Peters

Companion Press
P.O. Box 351
Shippensburg, PA 17257

ISBN 1-56043-410-4

For Worldwide Distribution
Printed in the U.S.A.

Acknowledgments

Paul the Apostle said of his contacts with people, "I am debtor to the wise, and to the unwise..." He said that he had learned from everyone whose life had come in contact with his own, and therefore was a debtor to each.

I believe that this is true for every person, for who has not learned something from his/her contacts with the people whose lives have touched their own? I have learned so much in this way, from all of the people that I have met, that I feel indebted to every one of them, be they friend or stranger. Therefore, I have become debtor to those who oppose as well as the ones who give encouragement, since the experiences I've had with them have taught me so much about life. Some have shown me how to live, and others, well, they have shown me how not to live. So, I acknowledge here that I remain indebted to every person whose life has in any way touched mine.

I am indebted to my children, Nancy & Barry, Jim and Patti, Sally & Lee and Patti Jane & Joey; and to my grandchildren Jason and Aubrey. All of them have provided much of the inspiration for my poetry.

I am certainly indebted to my parents, whose love for poetry and music was instilled in all 6 of their children at a very early age; and whose faith was transmitted to me almost before I could talk.

I am forever indebted to my sisters, Wanna, Georgia and Melva for the wonderful times of laughter, tears, memories, and just good fellowship that we have enjoyed over the years. The "Singing Grandmothers" may never be known far and wide, but we have had many blessed times together, in sharing and caring for each other.

I am truly indebted to Cathy and Don Nori who have been of greater assistance than I can begin to say, in a monetary way, in encouragement and suggestions for format.

So, here is a "treasury" from my personal scrapbook, for you — whoever you may be — who have taken the time to read this. If it is a blessing to one person, then it is worth the effort it has taken to bring it to fruition as a published work.

Dedication

To Sally — who believed in me, and whose constant encour-agement and help in the preparation of the manuscript probably brought this book to its completion.

About the Author

I have the good fortune of knowing this author, such a kind and gentle person, who has been blessed with the ability to put her most personal thoughts in print. While she would be certain to say that she has benefited from knowing us, it is truly we who are blessed by having her touch our lives.

As you read the author's uplifting and heartwarming works, notice how easily you identify with her feelings. As you read, take a deep breath...pause...close your eyes...and understand what she is saying. Her works are so sensitive and so refreshing!

While *MEMORY, GOD'S GOLDEN WINDOW,* is a joy to read, an even greater joy is personally knowing the author behind the pen. Though the business world knows the author as my Administrative Assistant, we really both work for each other. After you read, *MEMORY, GOD'S GOLDEN WINDOW,* you will then know what a special privilege it has been for me to have her touch my life.

M. Eugene Miller
Chief Operating Officer & Secretary
Valley Insurance Company

Memory, God's Golden Window

By Zelda M. Peters

Go to the Ocean

When there is time for me to take vacation
There's no place more inviting in the nation;
Than the ocean, where upon its sandy shore,
I love to walk and listen to its roar.
The vastness of this water in its bounds
Still limited by our Father, so astounds —
That I must think how great our God, who's will
Can tell this mighty ocean, "Peace! Be Still!"

I go there to the ocean, and I know
Its crashing waves will not its bounds o'erflow
And in its restful, rhythmic music there,
I can relax and soon forget my care.
So strange it seems, that here along this foam
That moves and groans, my heart can fill with song.
The depths, the spray, the tides, the sky, a shell;
All put a quiet o'er me like a spell.

I think that every person needs to flee,
To where there is an ocean or a sea;
When cares are pressing in upon the soul,
To hear the mighty billows toss and roll.
To lie upon the sand and listen, too
As God tells that great body what to do.
To pick up little shells that once were home
To little creatures, now in ocean foam.

Now, somewhere far away, they left behind
Some little bits of beauty we could find;
To carry with us as we leave and thus,
To take a little "ocean" home with us.
I have such little shells now in my home;
And often in remembering there alone,
I close my eyes and hold them in my hand;
And I am by the ocean once again.

A Boy Needs a Dog

A boy like me needs a dog like Jakie
When he goes out to play;
He runs with me and plays real hard,
But he never runs away.

Sometimes at night when it's cold outside
I'll ask my Mom and Dad
To let him come inside awhile —
That really makes him glad!

I lie down on the floor with him,
His coat is soft and red;
And he makes the nicest pillow
For a little fellow's head.

When I go to bed and he's back outside
I can hear him bark and I smile;
I'm sure he's as glad as I that he got
To come in and play for a while.

I'm glad I've got a dog like Jakie
And happy as I can be;
That I've got a Mom and Dad who'll let
Him come in and play with me.

Five Years Old

My birthday was on Tuesday, and I had a lot of fun;
My Mommie baked a cake and asked a lot
of friends to come.
The toys and books that I received
from Superman on down;
I never could have enjoyed — when I was One.

There was a Play-Doh factory,
with dough of every hue;
You stick the play-doh in and push and it
comes back to you.
I made hamburgers, shakes and fries,
in colors red and blue;
I never could have done that — when I was Two.

Then we all played with punch balloons
and jumped around for joy;
The grown-ups even laughed and played with me!
I saved Superman from mean old Loo-Thor(?)
I couldn't have done THAT — when I was Three!

Last year my cookie monster cake
was great — and it was blue;
And I had lots of friends come to my door.
We played some games and did the things that
"little kids" can do
When they are Four.

On Tuesday someone said to me,
"And just how old are you?"
I told him that this year I had turned five;
I know the folks all wonder how I feel about *this* age —
I think it's really great to be alive — and be Five!

My First Day of School

I'm all dressed up this morning,
and I thought I was prepared;
I've known this day was coming,
but I'm just a little scared.
I'm five years old — a little more,
and when the bus comes 'round,
I'm getting on, because today,
I'm Kindergarten bound.

I hope I'll see some of my friends
I knew at Day Care Center;
This is a kind of frightening world
that I'm about to enter.
My Mommie told me to be good,
and listen to my teacher;
If anything goes wrong, she knows my Mom,
and where to reach her.

My Daddy said I'm getting big
and school will be such fun;
But I think I'll really be quite glad,
when the first day there is done.
I'm going to miss old Jakie,
and I know he'll miss me too;
There's not another dog
who understands the things I do.

My baby sister is too young
to realize I'm going.
But it will be so quiet,
she'll suspect there's something doing.
While I'm at school I hope that she
will sleep a lot today;
So when I come back home this afternoon,
she'll want to play.

(Continued)

My First Day of School

(Continued)

The nest of birds outside our porch
may leave while I am gone;
But Mommie says they're learning too,
to fly out of their home.
They have to learn the way I do,
the things that birds should know;
I have to learn to read and write,
and that's why I must go.

I know already how to count
and write my numbers, too;
My abc's are easy,
I can sing them all for you.
My bus is coming, I must go,
but miss me when I leave;
And have a snack awaiting me,
when I come home, Mom, please!

Aubrey Rae

Someone's made a journey
from the hand of God above;
Someone's come to bless our hearts
and warm them with her love;
Sweetest little baby girl,
"What's her name," you say?
A pretty baby needs a pretty name —
she's Aubrey Rae!

Pretty little dimpled cheeks;
tiny little toes;
Soft blue eyes and auburn hair;
tiny button nose.
When you see her, you'll agree,
she's a special person;
Meant to brighten up the lives
of Mommie, Dad and Jason.

Hungry all the time, you bet —
but she's always fed;
And diapered, bathed and cuddled,
before she goes to bed.
And when she's fast asleep —
we all go to see her there;
We know that she's a gift from God;
We thank Him then in prayer.

What mystery! What wonder!
How marvelous God's love!
For who on earth could ever match
this gift from Heaven above?
For all the joy this little one
will bring we praise His name;
We'll do our best to guide her steps
that she may do the same.

My Sister

I used to be the only child,
and I was lonely too;
Until my parents told me there
would be somebody new;
They ordered from the angels,
a tiny baby sister,
And just as soon as she arrived at home,
I up and kissed her.

She smiles at me and every day
I show her toys and books
But so far she is still so small
that she hardly ever looks;
But oh, how much I love her,
and I watch her grow each day;
Waiting for the time she understands
the things I say.

I sometimes get to hold her
and she likes it when I do;
But if she cries I tell my Mom,
"I'll give her back to you."
It won't be very long before
she's two or three or four,
And then we'll play together —
I'll be lonely never more.

I'll teach her how to throw a ball
and how to ride a bike;
And if I am allowed,
I'll take her on a little hike.
I'm ever so much happier, now
that I'm an older brother;
I'm glad we got a baby girl —
for me and Dad and Mother.

If I Had My Way
Every Day Would Be Christmas

Everybody smiles and says, "Hello!"
Even grown-ups' faces are aglow —
We all have secrets that we have to keep;
And happy things to dream of when we sleep.

We get a nice big tree to decorate
And then the gifts! Oh, I can hardly wait —
To see what Santa brings — one thing I know;
We better get a lot of shiny snow.

And he can bring his reindeer and his sleigh
And jingle bells can jingle all the way;
It's so much fun when people everywhere,
Show other people that they really care.

I bet you know — by now it should be clear;
Why I'd like Christmas every day ALL YEAR!

The reason that the whole world on this day
Gives gifts to others, I have heard them say;
Is that once long ago a baby boy
Was sent to earth from Heaven to bring True Joy.

He was God's gift to us to make us good —
So we could do the things we know we should;
His name is Jesus, and the whole world sings
His praises as the greatest — King of Kings!
I like the songs about Him, for you see —
One time He was a little boy like me;
He knows how little boys like me need love,
And watches over us from Heaven above.

I bet you know — by now it should be clear
Why I'd like Christmas every day ALL YEAR!

The Balloon Launch

Vacation Bible School is here —
excitement fills the air;
I'm five years old, and so this year,
I'm glad that I'll be there.
On Sunday morning after church,
we met in a big room;
Where each of us was asked to help,
by launching a balloon.

Our names on tags, and news about
our Bible School were tied
To each balloon, before we took them
and all went outside;
The wind was blowing — sun was high —
'twas such a lovely day!
Then Ron said, "GO!" we let them loose,
and watched them sail away.

Some caught in trees and others sailed
away into the sky;
We hope that someone finds them and
will write us by and by.
Perhaps someone will read our note
and come to Bible School;
It surely would be great if all
the rooms and chairs were full!

We learn about a lot of things
that children ought to know;
Of how God loves us, and how we can
let His great love show,
To other children, so that they
will want to know Him too.
I think that Bible School is just fantastic,
now, don't you?

Six Years Old

A certain little lad I know,
is six years old today.
He's a very special little boy,
in almost every way.
And when he comes to my house
to visit for a while;
It makes me very happy;
he can always make me smile.

I wonder if you know the name
of this very special person?
I guess you do, but anyway,
I'll tell you: His name's Jason!

You say you knew it all along?
And you just played my game?
I'll tell you — kids in Grandma's day
and yours — they're not the same!

I think that even tho' you knew,
but didn't want to say;
I'll still say "Happy Birthday!
And have a Happy Day!"

What Is Christmas?

It's snowflakes swirling around my head,
and frolicking at my feet;
It's giving a smile and greeting to everyone I meet;
Christmas is thinking of others, whoever they may be;
Who have less of an abundance than my family or me.

Christmas is the little ones, with wide and happy eyes —
Trying to find out if Santa is really Daddy in disguise.
It's tying bright red ribbons on packages for the tree;
And telling inquisitive youngsters,
"You'll just have to wait and see!"

Christmas is cantatas, and carolling 'round the town!
Bringing joy to everyone whose face might wear a frown;
Christmas cakes and candy
make the whole house smell so good!
I wouldn't give up Christmas, even if I could!!

But even more than all of this,
when Christmas bells now ring;
They herald in the birthday of our Saviour and our King;
The joy we feel, the love so real, are attributes that show —
Our giving emulates the Gift God gave us long ago.

So have a joyous Christmas,
with the ones you hold so dear;
You know it won't come 'round again, for another year.
I wish you every happiness that Christmas time can give,
And joy enough to last you for as long as you may live.

The Nap He Didn't Need

He didn't "need" to take a nap,
and so I let him play;
And skip the bath he always got
about this time of day.
But suddenly I noticed that
the house was very still —
I wondered, "Where did that boy go?"
and felt a little chill.
I quickly hurried to the place
where he was playing last;
And there the little fellow sat,
his eyes in sleep were fast!
In spite of all the grime and dirt
from his head clear to his feet —
He made a picture in my heart,
ineffably sweet.
I had his Daddy get the camera out
and take a shot —
And then I gently picked him up
and laid him on a cot —
To finish out his sleep —
which of course he didn't "need;"
But when he got awake again,
he was refreshed indeed!

The Handicapped Can

Who can take a phone call, get the message clear?
If she cannot walk, don't assume she cannot talk —
The Handicapped Can.
Oh, the handicapped can; the handicapped can
If you'll try you'll understand —
and then you'll both feel good.

Who can type your letters, faster than a breeze?
Wheelchair-bound or blind,
at this skill I know you'll find
The Handicapped Can.
Oh, the handicapped can — although they may not talk,
May not run or even walk — the handicapped can.

Who can build a building, be an engineer?
Even if it's clear, when you speak he doesn't hear —
The Handicapped Can.
Oh, the handicapped can; just give the guy the plan
Then stand back and watch the man —
The Handicapped Can!

Who can solve your problems? Who can lend an ear?
Though he may not see, I am sure you will agree —
The Handicapped Can!
Oh, the handicapped can; they know the things you need
Though they're blind they still can lead,
The Handicapped Can!

Isn't it fantastic! You need expertise —
It's right before your eyes, but it comes in a disguise —
THE HANDICAPPED, MAN!
Oh, the handicapped can — just think this message through
You've got work that they can do —
The Handicapped Can!

(Continued)

The Handicapped Can

(Continued)

Oh, when you need persistence, with any job at all —
There's a gal or guy, you can use if you will try
Think HANDICAPPED, man!
Oh, the handicapped can;
cause they do their work with pride
And make you glad you ever tried -
THE HANDICAPPED CAN!

The Intruder

A hint of Fall was in the air,
a little snake surmised —
He looked for some good shelter,
safe from the rainy skies;
He slithered through the grass until
a little shed he found;
A hole through its weather-beaten floor
made it accessible from the ground.

Inquiringly, he thrust his little head
up through the floor;
A fine big cardboard box was sitting
just inside the door.
"I think I'll take a look," he said,
"It can't do any harm."
And soon he snuggled down inside
some clothing soft and warm.

And then one day he felt the box
go rumbling from the shed;
He curled up tight and pulled the clothing
up above his head.
At last he felt the box go "thump"
and settle on the ground;
He bravely stretched himself and said,
"I think I'll look around."

He wriggled from his cozy bed
and squeezed out through the lid —
He heard a scream and right away,
wished that he'd stayed hid;
He's gone now, lost his comfy bed,
and dear knows where he'll stay;
But no one's going to search for him,
they're glad he's gone away.

(Continued)

The Intruder

(Continued)

The box still sits there, strong and stout —
nobody wants to bother;
Lest somewhere in its depths they find,
he had a bigger brother.
A snake is such a little thing,
and it would never seem
That something so insignificant
could make a lady scream.

But should I a snake encounter,
I haven't any doubt; I'd find
The strength to climb a tree,
and maybe not come out.
The Fall can come with chilly air,
and I'll not feel ashamed or mean
If I don't open up my home,
and take these slithering creatures in!

Inspired by my brave Aunt Bertha,
who survived the invasion of the snake.

October

"Jack Frost Came To Call"

Jack Frost came stealing into town, late one October night;
He painted all the windows and left the grass all white.
Next day the sun shone bright
and pungent wood-smoke filled the air;
All nature had a different look, after he was there.
(Yes, Jack Frost came to town.)

Porches in the neighborhood, dressed up for Halloween
Big, bright, yellow pumpkins, with fodder in between;
Goblins stealing 'round
with scary masks and robed in white;
Even Superman swooped down, and gave me such a fright!
(When Jack Frost came to call)

Tiny "knock-knocks" at my door often could be heard;
Sometimes these "spooks" said, "Trick-or-Treat"
And sometimes, not a word.
A dish of treats and goodies dwindled as the night wore on;
And it wasn't very long before most of it was gone.
(But Jack Frost came and stayed)

It's such a pleasant time when "little folks" will come to call —
It makes me glad when Jack Frost comes
to tell me that it's Fall.
Some folks don't share the spirit that pervades October's air;
When Goblins'll getcha if you don't take special care!
(But Jack Frost's not afraid)

It takes a lot of courage to dress up and go to call
On grown-ups that you aren't sure will want you there at all!
So — make a special effort to be pleasant — it will bring,
To many little "ghosts" adventures worth remembering!
(When Jack Frost's gone away)

On an October Night

I saw a great big Harvest Moon,
shining in the sky;
High above the old oak tree,
that I was standing by.
(on an October night)
A big old owl sat on the tree,
and he said, "Whoo — Whoo — are you?"
I thought I'd scare him off and so
I said real loud, "BOO! BOO!"
And then a big, black cat appeared;
she arched her back — said, "YEOWW!"
I went inside — 'cause I was getting
sleepy anyhow.
I'm not afraid of owls and cats,
or a witch a'riding on a broom,
I just feel kind of better
when I'm safe inside my room.
(on an October night)

Autumn

God knew that when the harvest days were past,
And all the fruits were stored away at last
We'd see the fields now brown and we would sigh
That now all nature seemed about to die.

So, He, in wisdom, painted all the trees
In clothes of such great beauty as to please,
That in this sweet decay of life, we'd find
Its loveliness would give us peace of mind.

For even though when Autumn days are past,
Will come the Winter's harsh and cruel blast;
While warm and sunny Indian Summer's here
We find that it's a favorite time of year.

I paused this morning, looking toward the skies
Where honking geese, announcing their "good-byes"
Caused me to halt in silent admiration
To watch them winging Southward in formation.

Another miracle from our God, we know!
Who else told geese that it was time to go?
Who warned the squirrels to gather in their food?
Or bears to hibernate deep in the wood?

So, I, when I behold, in awesome wonder
The "coming out" of Autumn in such splendor,
Thank God (since Fall still makes me feel quite sad)
For all the beauties given to make me glad.

Let's Not Talk Turkey

I heard some turkeys talking, and they plan to run away;
They said they'd heard some talk
about a Great Thanksgiving Day,
When people sit around and watch a giant turkey roast;
Each one of them deciding that he ought to have the most.

They call this being thankful, and they talk of being kind;
One turkey said,
"Their thankfulness just really blows my mind!"
They're calling a big meeting of their own to plot and plan
A way of keeping each of them out of the roasting pan.

I think it would be kinder far,
if folks would watch their talk,
And try to keep it quiet if they're near where turkeys walk;
I'm not so sure that I can now enjoy that royal spread
Knowing that to set it out means some poor turkey's dead.

I think I might go shopping for a large zucchini squash;
You never have to kill them,
just stuff them when they're washed —
And come to think of it — don't know what stuffing to put in
If I used meat of any kind, I'd be in dutch again.

Why don't we each perform our favorite culinary feats —
Without a trace of any bird or other kinds of meats.
And then when our Thanksgiving Day is over, we, at least
Will not feel guilty to have slaughtered
some poor harmless beast.

(But for myself, I think I'll hurry to the grocery store
For one of those deep-frozen birds;
I'll look for one I'm sure
Has never heard the rumors that these other turkeys say
Are being circulated — I'll enjoy Thanksgiving Day!)

You Came to Me

You came to me, when I felt all alone;
The dearest in this world to me was gone.
You clasped my hand, and smiled through tears that day,
And there is nothing I can ever say;
That adequately tells how much of care —
Was lifted when I looked — and saw you there.

Mom's Last Trip

T'was on a warm and sunny day my Mom went on a trip;
She didn't buy a ticket, or book passage on a ship.
She didn't need to get prepared, she did that long ago;
Her Pilot called, and said, "My dear, it's time for you to go."

It happened very quickly, and she was not afraid;
To travel thro' the valley, for the Lord her fears allayed.
What wonder and what beauty she's beholding! And some day,
I want to take the trip she took, and there forever stay.

I know that she'll be waiting and watching for me there;
We'll have long talks as we did here —
there'll be so much to share.
There'll be no tears in Heaven, no sorrow, grief or pain;
But joy eternal, love supernal will forever reign.

I'll tell her how I tried to live for Christ and carry on;
Despite the sorrow that I felt, after she was gone.
When I have reached my sunset, don't think my life is lost;
Eternal life was bought for me, at a tremendous cost.

Mom told me of the Savior's love, when I was very young;
In stories from the Bible, and the many hymns we've sung.
I thank the Lord for seeing fit, to give me one so wise,
To guide my steps and help me find
a home beyond the skies.

"Honor thy father and thy mother..."

In October 1978

It was such a lovely October day,
when Mom and I started to Ohio to stay
for a week, for a visit With loved ones back home;
and the journey was pleasant,
for I was not alone.

We made it as leisurely a trip as we could;
looking at everything — as we always would
when we went for a drive, or topped a big hill;
we would just gasp for breath,
and our hearts just stand still!

We'd say, "Eye hath not seen, nor have we been told,
of all of the glory that Heaven will hold;
but if it's more beautiful than what's in our view —
I can't wait to get there — how about you?"

But the nearer we got to our "home" back there,
the more we would hurry — it lifted our care,
to know that again we would visit our friends
and sit with our loved ones — just see them again!

So when we arrived at Bertha's that night,
we were welcomed so lovingly, and we were a sight!
It had started to rain and we'd stopped for the night;
but the price was so great, we just zoomed out of sight.

And our clothes were all wrinkled
from the rain and the trip —
but Bertha just hugged us; she didn't mind one bit.
We had something warm and were so glad to be there;
we relaxed and had so much of life's things to share.

We went on to Woodrow's for breakfast next day,
and Marilyn fixed dinner before we got away;
and we listened to tapes and laughed quite a lot
at things we had said that we'd almost forgot.

(Continued)

In October 1978

(Continued)

Then we went to Melva's to visit a while,
and soon here came Woodrow with a message and smile;
he said Georgia called and wanted us to come,
so we soon said "good-bye" and started back home.

We stopped to see Georgia and had a nice chat,
and went back to Bertha's house right after that.
The next day we went to see Marshall and Mark,
and their friendly old dog who does nothing but bark.

Wanna and Harry and Josephine came,
and with them were Scotty and Jim, Josephine's man;
Mary stopped too, and we sang lots of hymns,
and listened to Mark play the organ again.

The day was still lovely, and we all looked so fair,
that we took lots of pictures of everyone there;
I have one that Wanna sent right after that —
and we all looked real good — but most of us fat!

We saw all Mom's brothers and sisters this time,
and I saw in her dear eyes, a special joy shine;
she'd longed for a visit with each one of them,
before someone left her and went on to Heaven.

I treasure that visit — we drove back, we two,
and I told Mom, "It's better, when I'm traveling with you;
the road was so lonesome when I used to drive "home",
but that was when I had to drive it alone."

Now, Mom's gone to Heaven, and I thought I would die,
just to think of my loss, and often I'd cry;
until late one Sunday, I asked God
to take the grief that I carried for it was too great.

(Continued)

In October 1978

(Continued)
He directed my attention to a worn old hymn book
which lay on my night stand, so I took a look.
The hymnal was published in 1879
and was meant to bring comfort to hearts such as mine.

I read the old hymns and I let Mom go free;
and a light seemed to shine and a voice said to me,
"Your Mom isn't dead, she has just gone away,
and with angels in Heaven, she is living today."

"Away where she's happy and sings all day long,
with the angels in Glory, their triumphant song,
of how she has finished her work here below;
and Jesus on her a bright crown did bestow."

The road will grow weary, at times, I am sure;
and I'll weep as I miss her and our good times of yore;
but one day I'll see her on Heaven's bright shore —
where none of us ever grows old anymore.

"looking for that blessed hope..."

A White Flower

This year is the first time since you have been gone,
that Mother's Day's come, Mother, dear;
I've always worn flowers in honor of you,
but I'll wear a white flower this year.

I'll wear a white flower for you;
remembering your love as I do;
When I go to the Mother's Day service this year,
I'll wear a white flower for you.

It just isn't real to me yet that you've gone,
to be with our Lord inthe sky;
I'll wear my white flower in memory of you,
but I'll see you again by and by.

I'll wear a white flower for you;
remembering your love as I do;
When I go to the Mother's Day service this year,
I'll wear a white flower for you.

White flowers were never your favorite, I know;
and I liked bright flowers, like you;
But white is the color that stands on this day,
for Mothers beyond the bright blue.

I'll wear a white flower for you;
remembering your love as I do;
When I go to the Mother's Day service this year,
I'll wear a white flower for you.

Clouds

Have you ever watched the clouds
as they go sailing through the sky of blue;
Upon a sunny Autumn day,
when breezes seem to speak to you?

Have you gone where, alone with God,
you feel washed free from every care;
And where your spirit feels renewed,
to find an inner solace there?

Today as I went walking
for a little time away, alone;
I looked up to the heavens,
and the glory of the sun that shone;

I felt such joy well up within,
at what my eyes beheld just then,
I wanted to keep walking on,
to drink that beauty fully in.

Oh, Autumn days, with sunny skies,
and winds that lift my spirits high;
Will bring me pleasant memories,
when Winter's here and snowflakes fly!

The Dove of Peace

My heart is bowed in sorrow, and the song
I used to have within my heart is gone;
The dearest friend I had in this whole land
Is living now, beyond the golden strand.

My heart is sore; my eyes with tears are wet
Remembering how I loved her, and as yet
No fellowship I share with any other
Has filled the void since I have lost my Mother.

When sorrow bows my head and grief sweeps in
Upon my soul, and I to tears am given
It's then the Dove of Peace comes close to me,
To heal my broken heart and set me free.

And time, I've heard, will soften all our grief,
And give to hearts made sad a sweet relief;
Not so, I find, for every passing day,
I seem to miss her more since she's away.

I've asked the Lord to tell her that I care
And miss her while I travel here and there;
On highways, byways, anywhere; it seems
It's always somewhere that we two have been.

The sunrise always took away our care
We watched it often, knowing God was there;
And once, upon the ocean's shore so old,
We watched the sun turn ocean blue to gold.

Together, we two watched life's setting sun
Until her race with life was almost run.
Now, lonely, I would give most anything
If I could once again just hear her sing.

(Continued)

The Dove of Peace

(Continued)

Her eyes tho' dimmed by age, her silvery hair
Were precious, as she dozed there in her chair;
And now and then it almost seems that she
Is not so very far away from me.

I'm sure the Dove of Peace, who gives me song
When life seems futile and when things go "wrong"
Will keep the promise He to me has given
That I will see my Mother soon, in Heaven.

The Dove of Peace, with Healing in His wings
Has come to me, and all life's broken things
Seem nothing more than dust, my heart is lighter
His healing makes life's dreary road seem brighter.

"The Dove of Peace shall come, with Healing in His wings."

"Blessed are they that mourn, for they shall be comforted."

My Body Is Shot

It's often been said that you're only as old
as you feel, and I truly agree;
My body is shot, but I tell you, I'm not!
My spirit is still young and free.

It hinders me some to walk with a cane,
when my legs don't perform as they ought;
But the truth of the matter is not that I'm old —
it's only my body that's shot.

My spirit is young, and the things that I've done
are not all I'd like by a lot
But it isn't ambition I lack, not at all;
it's this wreck of a body I've got!

So when I go limping around and you think
that I'm old, let me tell you, I'm not!
I'm doing the best that I can to stay young;
it's this body I'm dragging that's shot.

I get just a little disgusted each time
that I take the thing in for repair
It's just like an old Model T with a flat
that never can hold enough air.

So don't be surprised if I up and move out
and they put this old "bod" in a plot!
I'll get me a new one, and never again
will be stuck with a body that's shot!

Consider the Acorn

From the tiny little acorn
Grows the mighty, towering oak;
Where from a bow, the great old owl
Did those wise words evoke.
So when you labor long and hard
And accomplishments seem so few
Remember that the mighty oak
Was once a nut like you.
The acorn, dying to itself,
In the earth's bed damp and warm
Produced the great and mighty tree
To shelter owls from harm...
Or else perchance to furnish
The wood to build a home
Where happy people gather
And little children roam.
So if you are discouraged
That your work brings little gain;
Try dying out to self
And you will never be the same.
Look often to the acorn
And ever as you do —
Remember, you are able
For what any nut can do.

Skyways

To Aunt Bea, who got me up in the air.

When the evening sun is sinking
at the closing of the day
And I'm up above the clouds,
heading out Urbana way;
There's a feeling of excitement
as the jet-plane zips along,
And in my heart there's happiness,
and on my lips a song!

Though the airwaves may get turbulent
and tho' something may go wrong
With the Allegheny airplane
that will carry me along —
When I'm getting kind of nervous,
and am really wondering why
I had such a silly notion
to go sailing through the sky —

There's a thought that comes to cheer me,
and it comforts all my fear;
That it won't be long before I sit
and talk with you, my dear.
So I'm sending you this poem,
just to kind of let you know,
That I'm awfully glad you helped me
to decide that I would go.

It will be so short a visit,
and there's so much to be said
That I try to think of everything,
'till I'm dizzy in the head.
Maybe I'll keep still and listen;
this I cannot promise you —
Because listening is something
that I find so hard to do.

(Continued)

Skyways

(Continued)

It's been months since I have seen you
and I've missed you such a lot
So get out the instant coffee,
and your little water pot.
I have never seen a time
when we've run out of things to say
'twould be the same, I think,
were we together every day.

I want to see each one of you,
and record whoever I can;
Then when I am at home I can
enjoy this trip again.
I'll bring some tapes to play for you —
some funny and some sad,
Of joys we've shared and tears we've shed
on visits that we've had.

When we have said "good-bye"
and I have started home again,
I know my heart will feel
a very natural kind of pain;
But oh, how glad I am you're there;
and that we still can know
How much we're loved and needed
as we spend our days below.

Some day we'll take Flight F-I-N-A-L
to Heaven's shore;
We'll have a glad reunion,
and our partings will be o'er.
My fame and fortune (that I've missed)
won't matter over yonder;
This ought to give us something good
over which to ponder.

(Continued)

Skyways

(Continued)

Get ready for my "come down";
it was bound to happen, dear,
I've had that "puffed up" feeling
now for just too long, I fear.
I'm really not afraid of flying,
and on that you can bet —
Besides, they have assured me,
no one's been left up there — yet!

Moving

I moved again the other week
and said, as oft' before,
"I hope and pray with all my heart
that I shall move no more."

My things were packed away so good
in boxes nice and neat;
But it all had to be unpacked,
or else I couldn't eat;

Or change my clothes, or make a bed —
it was one tiresome chore;
And so, I really, truly hope
it happens nevermore.

I'm living near my children now,
we'd been so far apart;
We couldn't often visit, and
that nearly broke my heart.

Now sometimes in the evening
they drop in for a chat;
We laugh and talk and have nice times,
I really fancy that!

There'll come a day, I know that's true
when I'll move one time more;
Then I'll not need to pack my things,
or rent a place to store.

For I'll be going home at last —
my treasures are all there;
There'll be no bill for moving,
and I'll have no load of care.

I'll wait and watch from Heaven's Gate
with loved ones gone before;
To greet you where we'll never part
on that Celestial Shore.

A Quiet Place

Come walk with me, and let me hold your hand —
We'll walk where there's a place I like to stand;
A place where in my cherished solitude,
I find a sweet communion with my God.

See, here it is; a quiet little place;
(So near and yet so far from teeming pace)
That soothes the weary one and lets him feel,
And know, and find the values that are real.

Let's come here, you and I, sometime again
Away from life's dark problems and its din;
Let's talk to God and in communion find
True peace, that strong and everlasting kind.

My hideaway may be out on a hill —
Or by a little rippling stream or rill;
Or even in my home; the world shut out —
Wherever God can speak without a shout.

Too hurried, often, by our life's sick race
Are we, to stop and look into His face;
Who quiets all the storms and calms the sea
That often seems too much for you and me.

And if a quiet place you have not sought;
Begin today to seek it, and you ought
To walk there with the troubles of the day,
And watch them as they dim and fade away.

"In quietness and confidence shall be your strength."

Memories

The woman sat with folded hands;
rocking and remembering yesterday —
yes, it was yesterday;
it couldn't have been twenty years ago,
that they were here — playing around her feet;
and now they were gone!

Gone where?
Couldn't she somehow persuade them to come back?
Today she would have time to play with them —
there were no little shirts to mend.

But they were gone a long way,
down a pathway called "Time."
They could not return to her,
even if they heard her call —

Somewhere, deep inside, something hurt,
remembering the pleading voices;
"Please, Mama, play with us —
just for a little while?"

A tear dropped on the folded hands —
as she sat —
rocking — and remembering.

Musings of a Mama

A lovely house on a lovely hill,
with flowers bright and gay;
Sparkling windows and polished floors,
with nothing in disarray —
Would hardly be like a home to me —
'twould be lonely I truly fear;
Without some clutter and dust
that said there were little children here.

Smudges on door frames and
cookie crumbs on a rug that's worn from play,
A big old dog who comes right in,
to see if he gets to stay;
Toys and books and cowboy guns,
scattered from hither to yon,
Innocent prayers from children's lips,
when the day is done.

Chatter and clatter as they grow up;
laughter and tears and song;
These are the things that keep a house
a truly happy home.
Lessons to learn and chores to do,
bringing complaints from some;
Bedtime that brings untroubled rest,
because all their work is done.

Loving and teaching and training our young,
bring blessings that can't be bought,
When in their later lives we see
the results of the things we've taught.
Standards to live by, a faith to guide,
love to bestow and receive —
Fruits of a labor we hope will provide
meaning by which to live.

(Continued)

Musings of a Mama

(Continued)

And even after the children have grown,
and married and moved away;
We still keep the playthings on hand
because we are sure they'll be back some day;
Bringing a livelier, noisier band,
to make the house ring with their cheer —
And Grandma can still see smudges and crumbs
all of the time they're here!

When I tidy my house and a choice must make,
which windows I will clean —
I leave until last, the ones with the prints
where little hands have been.
No matter how tired or weary I grow,
it makes all of life worthwhile —
If one little boy pops in to ask,
"Will you play with me for a while?"

"Children are an heritage of the Lord."

Look! and Listen!

Upon the mountains glistening with snow,
I gaze in early morning, and I know
The strength I gain as here I stand and pray —
Will keep me through the trials of the day.

I see a rippling brook; I hear its chatter;
And suddenly my problems do not matter.
A bird goes winging through the towering trees,
His joyous song has put my heart at ease.

I board a plane in blackest thunderstorm;
I feel its power as I'm heavenward borne.
Then streaking upward, piercing clouds asunder,
I see a land of beauty, filled with wonder!

Above the storm, the sun is shining bright;
"Just so, it is," I think, "life's darkest night,
Is only covered over by earth's sorrow,
That hides the wondrous joy of God's tomorrow."

At evening, I behold with thankful heart,
The beauty of the sunset; with a start,
A solemn realization comes to me —
God put these blessings here for all to see.

If, as we travel onward day by day,
We use our eyes and ears, we'll never say
This world is drab and sad and labor vain;
God's rainbow always follows life's dark rain!

"I will lift up my eyes to the hills
from whence cometh my help..."

These Are My Friends!

They've taken my blood; and restricted my diet;
Put me to bed and told me, "Be quiet."
Then come the pills that make me feel groggy,
And then the whirlpool that makes my feet soggy.

Then Doctor says, "Up on your feet! Take a walk —
And write on the floor with your toes." — but no chalk.
I'm promised some needles that enter the heel,
And go to the kneecap, I KNOW, I can feel!

The various other compassions they've shown
Are proof that each one has a scheme of his own
To vent his frustrations; but I must bear in mind
That each of these doctors is infinitely kind.

Yes, these are my friends, and it's my fervent prayer
That I never encounter an enemy somewhere!
But, I've noticed, in spite of this medical "pain"
I'm walking again, without using my cane!

Antiseptically dedicated to Drs. Cohen & Zlotoff

Rats!

(and mice)

It's easy enough to be happy
When everything's going real nice;
But the gal worthwhile is the one who can smile
When her home's been invaded by mice!

To live in a park where you cannot
Have a nice little dog or a cat
Is tragedy sure, which is hard to endure
When right under your sink is a rat!

Hats off to the wonderful woman
Who sat on her table all night
While the gnawing progressed, 'twas a terrible test
But the rodents she vowed she would fight.

Be proud of the lady of courage!!
Next day, with a gleam in her eye
She called for a man who said, "I surely can,
Feed them poison they'll *love*—and they'll die!"

And that night she waited with pleasure
For the patter of those little feet;
They ate until they could scarce walk away
And soon were stretched out nice and neat.

It's easy enough to be happy, for sure,
When everything's going so sweet;
But the gal worthwhile is the one who can smile,
When the rodents come inside to eat.

There's a Mouse in the House

I know a young woman named Nancy
Who to most animals takes a fancy
But she grew very pale at the words of her spouse
When he said, "There's a mouse — in the house!"

Now kittens and puppies are bigger
But nothing is very much quigger
Than Nancy's retreat, at the words of her spouse,
"My dear, there's a mouse—in the house!"

The sight of a trap makes her sick,
She says, "Get it out of here, quick!"
But the grin on his face makes her wroth at her spouse
When he says, "There's a mouse — in the house!"

Reach out Today

A lady sits by her window today,
Hoping that someone will come her way;
Perhaps to stop for a little while
And bring her joys that will make her smile.
Her face is lined and wrinkled and old,
And a tear goes trickling down a fold
In her dear kind face, as she sits today
Waiting for someone to pass her way.

This home for the aged is nice and clean
But it's been so long since she has been
Any place outside these walls;
And she does get tired of walking the halls.
She sees others there, and she will spend
Time in trying to make a friend;
So that the hours will pass away
A little pleasanter today.

Who is this dear lady, don't you know?
She's somebody's mother, yes, that's so;
And somebody's mother would like to see
Her children, and she'd happy be,
If someone would come and take her a ride,
And tell her they loved her, and then tried
To show that love in little ways
To ease the passing of her days.

May God watch over them! Moms and Dads
While they live in memory of what they've had;
And may some children whose lives were blest
By having such parents to train for each test,
Remember the times they were young and sure
And able to do and to endure.
May they visit and reach out in love today;
Tomorrow they may have passed away.

"Honor thy Father and thy Mother"

There'll Come a Day

There'll come a day when earthly ties are severed,
And we shall be at home on Heaven's shore;
There'll come a time when partings will be finished,
And we'll say no "good-byes" forevermore.

When night has pinned aside her blackest curtain,
And we see clearly and can understand;
The way our Saviour led us was the best way
How glad we'll be we walked the path He planned.

How trifling then will be our greatest worry
How insignificant our direst straight;
Once we have crossed into that land oft longed for
And looked at what's beyond the pearly gate.

By using every word we could, we'd falter
If trying to best describe what we shall be;
Or the things our Father has prepared to give us
That shall be ours thro' all eternity.

If we could see beyond this veil of sorrows
Our hearts would lift and songs of praise we'd sing;
God's word says that we can not e'en imagine
The joy we'll know when we have seen our King.

When trials sore oppress and life seems useless
Remember, friend, there'll come a day — some day;
When all these heavy burdens that distress us,
Will be forgotten, banished, gone for aye.

Lift up your head, and praise when you are burdened
The Devil cannot stand your praise to hear;
He'll flee, should you the blood of Christ just mention
And you will feel God's presence very near.

For the joy Paul spoke of, that awaits us yonder
We dare to face our hardest trials here;
That in that lovely land for which we're striving
Our God shall wipe away our every tear.

> "Weeping may endure for a night
> but joy cometh in the morning."

I Have an Appointment

(That I Shall Keep)

I have an appointment I must not forget
With a dentist in my home town;
I know the day and hour, of course
And will go when the time comes 'round.

And other appointments I shall make
As I travel along thro' the years;
Some that I make will bring me joy
While others may bring me tears.

But there's an appointment (that I shall keep)
And the hour I do not know;
I may be awake, or I may be asleep
But either way, I shall go.

There'll be no planning or rushing around
I've had years to get prepared;
It's a trip I will make, and I know not when
But I'm not one little bit scared.

I have my appointment book right at hand
With instructions to guide me right;
In order that there is no question at all
When I'm ready to take my flight.

And this appointment (that I shall keep)
Is only a one-way trip;
I'm on "stand-by" status, so I'm alert
And ready to board that "ship".

The Captain is charting the course for me
So I have not a worry or care;
I'm just to go on with my life and hear
When He calls me to meet Him somewhere.

So, I have an appointment (that I shall keep)
And I'll be happy to go;
Because the appointment (that I shall keep)
Is with God (if you didn't know).

"It is appointed unto man...once to die..."

Go Softly

A baby girl, sent straight from Heaven
To parents proud this child was given
They said, "Sh-h-h she's asleep."

She learned as she was expected to
The darling tricks that babies do
But — sh-h! She's asleep.

First she crawled, and then she stood
And walked so soon, they knew she would;
Go softly — she's asleep.

Then to school, this lovely child went
Always happy and well content
And angels kept her safe.

A few years passed, she grew so tall
It didn't seem possible at all
That she'd grown up so fast.

Then she married and children came
And she loved them just the same
As she was loved.

Then they grew up and moved away
And the house is lonely now today.
She misses them so much.

Then a widow, tears now pour
From eyes so shiny bright before;
And sorrow bows her head.

Nodding there in her chair is she
With a furrowed brow and aching knee;
Go softly — she's asleep.

An angel came one day about eleven
And took this dear one home to Heaven
Her voice no more I'll hear.

(Continued)

Go Softly

(Continued)

But over in Heaven's lovely land
She's been united once again
With those she sorely missed.

It's true that life's like flowers fair
And all too soon they aren't there;
Where did the years all go?

Go softly, ask the angels to keep
Your precious aged as they sleep;
They'll soon awake in Heaven.

A Letter

When I go home from work each day
And I'm a little weary
If there's a letter in my mail
It always seems to cheer me.
A letter brings me news from those
Whose faces I seldom see
And they always say they'd like to have
Another letter from me.
And when I think how glad I am
That someone took the time
To write a letter just for me
I want to write a rhyme
That tells each one how much it means
To hear from friends away
And how it always cheers my heart
And brightens up my day.
Is there a letter you should write
To one who might be blue
And who would instantly cheer up
If he should hear from you?
Then sit right down, don't put it off
And write that little letter
And send it out across the miles
To one who'll feel much better
Just knowing there is someone yet
Who thinks of him and who
Will take some time to write to him
And tell him this is true.
A letter takes so little time
When once we start to write
And when it reaches its destination
It makes some heart feel light.

(Continued)

A Letter

(Continued)

I think of you, and often times
Can't tell you any better
Than when I sit right down at home
And write you a nice letter.
This letter comes with love from me
I hope will make you glad
Your letters are some of the nicest gifts
That I have ever had.

To My Children

I asked my God for children, and He gave me four to love;
To guide and teach and point the way to Heaven up above.
My world was incomplete before they came to bless my life.
The joy they brought made compensation
for the times of strife.

Too soon they grew to young adults and left my loving care;
But still I live in memory with the times that they were there.
One went to college, studied hard, and married a fine man,
And in their own home now they live,
and work and love and plan.
I'm justly proud of what they've done
and that they love the Lord
And study so that they may work for Him, and know His word.

My only son, has grown so tall, and married too, and he
Has such a fine, good son and daughter in his family.
Another daughter works quite hard, within an office now;
She's newly married, and I cannot ever tell you how
That little girl has moved my heart
with love and joy and cheer,
And she just grows more precious with every passing year.

My baby girl is all grown up and has a husband fine —
It can't be true that she's a wife — this little babe of mine!
Three sons-in-law, young men of worth are added to my clan
I love them all and try to be the best mother-in-law I can.
My daughter-in-law is still quite young,
and in my heart's a place
For her, whose life is busy with two youngsters to keep pace.

Sometimes a mother finds it hard to love each child the best
And yet be careful that she loves no one more than the rest.
Each child and child-in-law is different and, as so they be,

(Continued)

To My Children

(Continued)

Each one requires a different kind of mother-love from me.
May I be faithful to each one, and love them, come what may;
That when they older grow they each may look back and say;

"I well remember Mother's love, and tho' she's old — or gone;
The memory of her tenderness to me will linger on."
But Moms are human and they are not always what they seem;
But underneath what outward shows,
you'll find a love-light beam.
So while I'm here, I know that I will err and human be
But when I'm gone, I hope that they will fondly think of me.

A day will come, it won't be long, and may they understand
When I will go to be at home in Heaven's happy land.
And I would like for them to know that after I am gone;
The Bible says that all my prayers for them go on and on;
So may they put the Savior first, in all they strive to do,
And all the blessings that they need, will be provided, too.

Now I Live Alone

I live alone, now, Lord, and although I know that You
Are ever near, sometimes the way is filled with dread and fear.
My heart is filled with inner peace,
the kind that sees me through
And yet sometimes my heart cries out
for someone to be near.

I'm glad that you do not get tired of hearing, when I call
So many times I need your help when I have plans to make;
And tho I know that all the while your hand is over all
I still can sometimes feel my heart
from all my burdens quake.

So glad I am that when the shadows come and o'er me fall
I have an avenue of prayer to which I turn for strength
Though needs arise, I cannot fail when on your name I call
I know my needs will all be met and burdens eased at length.

Be near me Lord, when night draws near, if I am feeling sad
Let your great peace and comfort come to cheer me and to keep
And when I lie upon my bed within my home alone
I pray that you will give your angels charge so I can sleep.

Now, older I have grown, and as I think about the past,
I understand the way that you have led me has been best;
Determined now, am I, that trusting in your word alone
I'll be made adequate for every trial and every test.

Let love ones, those most dear to me, remember I am here
And when they think of me, may they be understanding too
That some day sooner than they think,
tho' youth they hold so dear,
They could be living quite alone, and trusting only You.

Let wisdom come to all who have not yet this time of life
Approached, that when they do
they'll learn to trust Thy love so true;
And may they understand,
before the brink of life they reach —
That older folks who seem so strange are really people, too.

I'd Like to Say

I wish that I could say
that I had sailed the seven seas —
And tell you all the lovely sights I'd seen;
I'd like to paint a picture with the words that I would use
So you would feel that where I was, you'd been.

I'd like to say that I had seen
the loveliest of sights —
Perhaps the different churches in each land —
I'd use descriptive language —
words would come at my command —
And you would feel we'd been there, hand in hand.

If I had been to visit in exotic desert lands —
I'd paint a picture of those mysteries;
Where no rain falls, but flowers bloom
and cactus fills the land
With beauties that no other place you'd see.

But I have seen some other things
that I can best describe —
Just picturing — again in my own mind.
The beauty of a sunset over ocean's mighty deep —
Such sunset at no other spot is seen.

I've walked along the beaches
of these mighty tossing waves —
I've picked up little shells upon the shores;
Amid life's wild commotion
I have found a peace so sweet —
It bids me come when trouble o'er me pours

And I have walked along a rippling crystal mountain stream —
I've sat on rocks and closed my eyelids there;
I've felt the breezes,
smelled the little mountain flowers, too
And there again I've left my every care.

(Continued)

I'd Like to Say

(Continued)

God gives to us, wherever we are,
His beauties to enjoy
In each there is the mystery of His love;
And if we look and listen,
as we walk along life's road —
We'll find our hearts are lifted up above.

Tho' trials or the problems
that perplex us every day —
Engulf us and surround us like a shroud —
We'll find release and comfort
as we look at what He gave —
And soon we'll feel we're floating on a cloud.

Ten Little Birthdays

One little Birthday, for a little boy
All I had to do was buy a shiny toy;
Two little birthdays, getting bigger now
Has a little puppy, feeds him puppy chow.
Three little birthdays, where did the time go?
Such a busy little boy, always on the go!
Four little birthdays, gracious sakes alive!
Can it be that next year Jason will he five?
Five little birthdays; he has brought more joy
Never child was dearer than this little boy.
Six little birthdays, now he goes to school
Now he'll learn his numbers and the golden rule.
Seven little birthdays! He's in love with life —
Certain little neighbor's girl wants to be his wife!
Eight little birthdays, now he's moved away
Making some new playmates, growing more each day.
Nine little birthdays, and he's moved again —
Wonder where he'll be when he is finally ten?
Ten little birthdays! My that time went fast —
Now a big fourth grader — he grew up so fast!
But I know a secret, that I'll tell you here
It will never matter — his age, his height, career;
He's my favorite grandson...told him this before...
Every year he's dearer than he was before.

Bittersweet

Once, years ago, I drove along a quiet country road;
Enjoying all the wild flowers
growing where no blade had mowed.
Along the fences, there entwined were vines, a sight to meet;
It was the lovely wandering tendrils of the bittersweet.

I stopped my car, and walked to where I had a better view
And as I marvelled at such beauty, berries orange in hue;
My thoughts took wing, and in my marvelling I a lesson found
That in our lives,
tho' overgrown with clutter, there abound —

Some things that to us bitter seem, and other things so sweet
That in attempting to describe it, life seems bitter-sweet.
Without the rains that on us fall, we could not stronger grow
And we could not in joy abound, should we no sorrow know.

Along life's ways, where'er we go, we meet both joy and pain;
But always we can know that sunshine surely follows rain.
As years go by, although we sigh, when burdens bend us low
Our spirits soar, when we've endured our crosses,
and they go.

Into each life, this mixture comes,
and tho' sometimes we're sad,
Our trials make us stronger, as we take the good and bad.
Like that sweet vine, whose berries bright,
are bitter to the taste
Our lives are touched with bitter-sweet,
that we should never waste.

If we can look upon each trial, as holding for our good
A lesson that we otherwise had never understood;
Then we will drink our cup of life and never know defeat
Although the taste is something strange —
the taste is bitter-sweet.

Memory, God's Golden Window

When we are young, and filled with hopes so high
They tower far into the cloudless sky;
When we with strength unbounded, free from care,
Enjoy whatever pleasures we can share;
When with our childhood friends we live and grow,
We're building memories as on we go.
And memories are windows made of gold,
That look upon the past when we are old.

What time in childhood's shining hours is spent,
Becomes a hallowed book of memories lent;
When after youth is gone, and age makes slow
We look again through God's Golden Window;
A window to the past, with treasures rare,
When looking back, erases many a care;
To look ahead is frightening for the old,
So they look through God's Window made of Gold.

Do not upon the aged look askance,
If from their golden windows they perchance
Bring forth some cherished memory to share
If you should stop a while to visit there.
Remember, you are young; you look ahead,
With dreams and visions to your future led;
The aged dream of joys of yesteryears,
And to their future sometimes look with tears.

And further, there will come to you some day,
Quite suddenly, 'twill seem, from far away;
A memory of a day since past and gone,
And you will find the memory lingers on.
Then you will know the value of days past,
That printed on your memory joys to last,
When challenges of life are nearly gone;
God's Golden Window will help you travel on.

Christmas Blues

"Twas the week before Christmas and I didn't care —
No evidence of Christmas was seen anywhere;
No stockings were hung by the chimney with care
For a very good reason, no chimney was there.
The thermostat was turned to a cool 55
And the oil lamps were burning, I think there were 5
The gas tank was empty and so was my purse,
Yet somebody told me that things could be worse.
I looked in the refrigerator for something to cook
And there wasn't one thing — and I took a good look!
I got out some dried soup and heated the water
And then I sat down and drank a hot supper.
When out on the porch I heard a big "clunk"
The wind had reduced the storm door into junk.
I went out to pick up the fragments of glass
Slipped on the ice and fell flat on the grass.
I picked up my bruises and took them inside
And there in the kitchen immediately spied
An animal — 'twas only a little brown mouse
But he was running and jumping all over the house!
I got out a trap and set it just so;
Forgot it, but found it again — with my toe!
I had to do something and do it right quick
To cheer myself up — this stuff made me sick.
I decided to bake, so I got out a book
And for a good recipe started to look
I'll make some nice cookies," I started to mutter
When I remembered I hadn't the eggs or the butter.
I had a nice gingerbread mix on the shelf
I thought, "I'll make *something* in spite of myself!"

(Continued)

Christmas Blues

(Continued)

I mixed it all up and the oven was hot,
When I smelled something burning—the handle of a pot
I had stored in the oven, so I opened the door
And out of it black smoke started to pour
I opened the house to let the smoke out
And then I sat down and started to pout;
Since Christmas comes only one time in a year
You'd think something ought to go right around here!
When order was somewhat restored once again,
I poured the gingerbread mix into a pan
Put it into the oven with quite a tired sigh,
And thought, "I'll rest while it bakes,
I'm so tired I could die."
I lay down on the sofa and fell fast asleep
When choking and coughing I awoke with a leap
My gingerbread black from two hours of baking
Was a terrible sight for one just awaking
I tested the thing and found it so hard
I opened the door and threw it out in the yard!
My spirits are low, but I will not complain
— Unless someone mentions Christmas again!

P.S. On January 7th — and this is no bunk
The wind did reduce the storm door into junk!!!

"A merry heart doeth good...like a medicine."

The Dancers!
Song Without Music

"Under the Silvery Ball at Webster Hall"

The orchestra leader raised his hand,
and as with magic he struck up the band.
As the lovely melodies filled the air
the music seemed to remove all care.
And quite suddenly dancers seemed to pour,
upon the polished danceroom floor.

Watching, entranced, as they glided with ease,
to lovely music which each heart pleased
I watched one dancer who's heart was light,
dance the foxtrot with great delight.
Crossing steps with style so sure,
he glided smoothly across the floor.

In fascination I watched this guy,
who's lovely lady was deft and spry
A remarkable couple they were, I declare,
and they seemed to be dancing on nothing but air.
He whispered something in her ear,
but not so softly I couldn't hear.

"Were I to dance the whole night through,
my dear, I'd want to dance it with you."
Now the band struck up a Latin beat,
the Cha-Cha and they looked so neat.
But now my attention was quickly drawn
to a lovely lady who moved along
So light on her feet, so excitingly sweet,
and she kept me 'rapt with her dancing feet.

(Continued)

The Dancers!
Song Without Music

(Continued)

Oh, Dancing Lady, oh, Dancer, you're rare!
You've lifted my worries, and banished my care
The music changes, but you never do —
would that I danced as lightly as you.
The midnight came, and the music died,
and the dancers stopped and sadly sighed;
There's magic under the Silvery Ball,
that attracts us all to Webster Hall.
If you've never been there, come go with me,
and I am sure that you'll agree
No magic that you can imagine at all,
can compare with the magic at Webster Hall.

Broken Things

When I was small, I had a gift; 'twas given by my Mother
Two little dogs on a pink cushion, lying by each other;
I treasured that small gift, because it was from Mother dear
And when one day it fell and broke,
she dried my falling tear.
She glued the broken pieces and I could scarcely tell
That it was ever broken—she'd mended it so well.
Thro' passing years my Mother mended
other broken things —
Toys, or clothes, or broken hearts,
with glue or thread or strings
Or with an understanding heart, that knew the pain I bore
When glue or thread or strings
could just not fix things anymore.

And later on when she was old and she had need for one
To try to mend her broken things, as she had always done —
My heart remembered Mother's love, and so I tried to be
As understanding of her then, as she had been of me.
And when she had grown older
with Time's furrow on her brow
I hurt her feelings; tho' I did not mean to anyhow
I tried to understand the way she felt, and I am glad —
Our fellowship was soon restored, that we had always had.
Now she has gone to her reward; we're parted for a while
But I recall with joy the times I gave her cause to smile.

I'll always hear in memory, her singing 'round the home
And some glad day I'll join her as
we sing around God's throne;
And we will never saddened be by a word that hurts or stings
And we will never have a need to mend our broken things.

(Continued)

Broken Things

(Continued)

If we could know the time we have to finish out life's years
We probably would soon forget
the things that brought us tears —
And we would run to those whose hearts
are pained by sorrow's stings
We'd try to understand and help to mend the broken things.
If you are hurt by what you feel is cruel and thoughtless art
Perhaps the reason is, that loved one has a broken heart.
Try reaching out and laying down
the pride that hurts and stings —
It sometimes takes a lot of love to mend life's broken things.

I still have those small china dogs;
the cushion's long been gone —
But when I look at them today,
those memories linger on.

Across the Miles at Christmas

There never comes a Christmas
that my thoughts don't cross the miles
That separate me from my loved ones dear;
I burn my candles,
listen to the carols that "Bing" sings
And wish that I were there or you were here.

The years keep spinning past us,
and they really go too fast
For us to take the time we need to spend
With those we like to write to, or maybe even call
Our precious loved ones and our dearest friends.

This homely little poem comes to say I think of you
Though miles may separate us at this season
I'll think of you this Christmas
and picture in my mind
What you'll be doing, and that's just the reason

I'm writing you to wish for you
the most delightful time
You've had so far this year, and then to add
I pray that you will have
the very happiest New Year
Of any year that you have ever had.

And when I kneel to pray at night,
again I'll think of you
You're on my mind quite often, don't you see?
And when you pray, my dear ones,
it will mean so very much
If you will say a special prayer for me.

With God there is no distance separating us from Him;
He hears us all no matter where we are
And so, if He is with you there,
and yet is here with me —
We really aren't separated far.

I've Staked My Claim

Of earthly goods I have no store, my treasures here are few
But I have staked a claim to a mansion far beyond the blue;
And I can do without a lot to send up the material
To build a mansion beautiful in lands that are ethereal.
The building blocks are not cement or brick that you can see
I build upon the Rock — my Lord, Who bled and died for me.
My life, each day, if lived for Him, according to His plan
Pays dividends far greater than any bank here can.

Yes, I have staked my claim, away beyond the rolling tide
Of problems that sometimes would try
my treasures there to hide.
My Lord directs my life's affairs as on this road I tread
And nothing that can happen now
will fill my heart with dread.
He said, "I will go with thee," and so I do not fear
The while I'm holding to His hand, I feel His presence near;
I may not seem to friends of mine to have a lot of treasure
But in my mansion over there,
I've wealth I cannot measure.

My Lord instructed me to lay not up while I am here
My riches, where they could corrupt
and cause me constant fear;
That others might these treasures take,
who never knew the way
To purchase without gold or jewels, a truly better way.
If I would store up all my wealth it would with age corrode
And never bring me happiness, although I'd think it could.
I've staked a claim and though I may
seem poor and weak and old,
I have a mansion waiting me on streets made out of gold.

Going Home

The Fall has touched the Pennsylvania hills
And turned the foliage crimson, yellow, brown;
Thanksgiving's almost here and my heart thrills
Because I'm going back to my home town.

I've lived in Pennsylvania a long time
And have my children here not far from me.
But back in old Ohio, those of mine
Are calling me to come and I must flee.

We probably will sing some old-time hymns
And harmonize as we did long ago;
When Dad and Mom were with us — and again
We'll sing, for them, the old songs that we know.

Like "Rock of Ages" and "Hiding in Thee"
And maybe one Dad liked "I'll Fly Away"
So, this will surely be, at least for me —
A very, very grand Thanksgiving Day.

No matter where on earth I chance to go
When holidays come near I'll always be
Within my heart, at least, in O-hi-o
With those whose love means everything to me

We may not all be here another year
So while we walk this earth, as on we go
We ought to try to visit those most dear
And if we love them try to let them know.

Yes, I am going "home" and I rejoice!
God gave to me my loved ones to make glad;
My heart sings and I *must* give voice —
To singing — how could my heart now be sad?

Lost and Found

If you should see a little boy in blue jeans
And a little girl with honey colored hair,
Please let me know for seems as if I've lost them,
And I've been looking almost everywhere.

I saw them yesterday out in the meadow
Chasing butterflies and having fun,
And then last night I gave them each a big hug
And tucked them into bed when day was done.

Or could it possibly have been last Tuesday
Or maybe even twenty years or so —
I watched them playing 'round about the farmhouse
Not dreaming that some time they'd have to go.

The faded little blue jeans too, are missing
And also a small frock of calico;
I thought I'd have them here for such a long time
And never dreamed I'd ever miss them so.

So, if you see them, tell them I am waiting
And longing for the time that they'll return,
I'd love to make a plate of cookies for them
The kind they loved, with butter from the churn.

Oh, yes, I guess that they have simply grown up,
And soon will have small children of their own;
So I'll just keep on making all those cookies
To be in practice when they do come home.

Perhaps there'll be a little blue-eyed laddie,
In faded jeans and scruffy little shoes
And a little pig-tailed girl with gingham dresses,
Who'll hurry in to tell me all the news.

Oh, what a wonder! How that day will thrill me!
How shall I tell you just what it will mean,
To welcome once again some little children
To cheer my heart and make me young again!

And Now It's Autumn

I remember Spring, when little birds would sing
And butterflies sail high, into an azure sky;
No cares were pressing me, and happy as could be
I took the greatest joy with any little toy —
But too soon, Spring was gone.

Then magic Summer came; but things were quite the same
The sunny hours flew, with many things to do.
I took a husband fine, and little babes were mine
But they grew up so fast — I wanted time to last;
But Summer, too, took wings.

And now the Autumn's here, with golden mem'ries dear
To bless my life in ways not known in other days.
Grandchildren now are mine,
with bright blue eyes that shine.
My steps are growing slow, as onward I must go —
Soon Autumn, too, will pass.

Then Winter will be here; "the best of life," I hear —
When silver crowns my brow,
and 'neath life's load I bow:
But as I onward plod, I'm nearer to my God
Than I have been before, for when the Winter's o'er
Then Spring will come again.

And when Spring comes again, within a happy land
I'll watch the birds sail high, into an azure sky
And hear their happy songs, as I with angel throngs
Feel new life springing up, to fill my waiting cup —
And I shall live again!

"For we know that when the earthly tabernacle
of this flesh shall be dissolved, we have a house
not made with hands, eternal in the heavens."

Down on the Farm

I work in the city, and work very hard,
To my job I am almost a slave;
But in my day-dreaming I'm back on the farm,
Watching fields of ripening grain wave.
The warm summer days and the sun-drenched hours,
Spent "down on the farm" are to me,
The fondest of memories to which I lay claim;
Yes, there again I'd like to be.

The lovely nasturtiums around the old house,
The buzzing of big bumble bees;
And many refreshing and fun-filled hours,
I spent 'neath the evergreen trees.
They lined the old lane, and stood 'round the house
And in the night I heard them mourn,
As the winds swept their branches
and caused them to whine,
With a sadness that sounded forlorn.

Yes, down on the farm I would like to return,
To be part of a quieter life;
To drink in the fragrance of freshly mown hay,
And forget all the sadness and strife
That have come into being since I went away
And left the old farm, far to roam;
When I have a time for reflection, it seems,
I just simply want to go "home".

My Father's Hands

I remember the log house where I grew up
I remember the woods behind,
And the favorite places we children played
And when these things come to mind —
There is something else that I now recall
Much more than the house or lands;
I remember my hard-working father so dear,
And his calloused and work-hardened hands.

He rose up so early, before it was light
And was off to his work on time,
His wages were small, but he made them do
And Mamma could stretch each dime;
She made all our bread, I remember so well
How good it smelled when it baked;
And Dad would come home from his work at night
So tired that his whole body ached.

He would sit down to eat, and I can recall
When he picked up his fork and knife,
His hands were so brown, and calloused and rough
I'll remember it all of my life.
He loved Mamma's cooking and often said
She was the best cook in the world —
But I'll never forget how I felt when I saw
His hands so calloused and gnarled.

He had no fine clothing to dress for "good"
But I never heard him complain;
He went out to work in all kinds of weather
The wind, the sun or the rain.
And when it was evening and supper was o'er
He'd gather us 'round and we'd sing;
My Dad could play any instrument at all
So he'd play and we'd make the house ring.

(Continued)

My Father's Hands

(Continued)

But I can remember, and I am so glad —
(His footprints he left on the sands —)
The every line and scar that he had
On his rough and work-hardened hands.
And when I recall how times were back then
I think our respect he commands —
For all of the labor he gave in love
And the scars on his dear gnarled hands.

If I could but tell him since I have grown
That now I appreciate more,
The work that he did and the trials he knew
To keep the wolf 'way from our door;
I'd tell him how well I remember the things
That he did to meet all the demands —
That were placed upon him, and I'd say how I love,
The memory of his precious hands.

Mother — A Gift from God

When God created Mothers,
He was very careful in their distribution.
They were very precious in His sight,
and made of such unique substance
that He could trust them to care for His little ones.

A Mother is a special person
with love enough for many children,
time enough to hear
what each one wants to confide in her,
and wisdom enough to understand what is in each heart.
She loves each child "the best"...
but none better than the rest.
She makes each child feel most important to her,
without offending any of them.

She can sometimes read the thoughts of her child,
and put into words feelings the child
is unable to find words to express.

She has endurance that only a Mother can have...
strength enough to go without sleep for days
if her little one is ill and needs constant care.

A Mother loves God, kittens, puppies,
baking cookies, creating snacks
for bedtime or after school,
baseball, the Muppets and Superman.
She loves bedtime stories,
dot-to-dot pictures, coloring books,
P.T.A., Sunday School and Daddy...
not necessarily in that order.

When knees are scraped and pants are torn,
when socks don't match and toast is burned,
when grades are down and spirits, too,
and when a child's world comes tumbling down...

(Continued)

Mother — A Gift from God

(Continued)

there is one who can always work
a little "magic" that makes everything seem
not so upside-down.
She somehow knows how to put hope back
into a saddened heart.
We call her Mother, friend, helper,
worker of "miracles"...
God calls her "blessed."

When Mother gets older,
she isn't always so sure of herself.
Sometimes she can't remember even "little things."
Occasionally she drops things and breaks them,
or spills coffee at the table.
You can comfort Mother's heart
and make her feel very special
if you say, as she often said to you,
"Don't worry, everything will be all right."
Then you can put sunshine in her life,
a bright smile on her face,
and chase the dark clouds away,
simply by saying, "I love you, Mom."

Remember, your aging Mother was once young...
full of energy and bright hope.
Now, she lives with her fond memories.
If you can help to bring back
enjoyable memories of yesterday,
and share her nostalgia, you'll never be sorry.
When God calls her home to be with Him,
YOU will begin to understand what memories mean,
and what God was about when He created MOTHERS.

"Her children rise up and call her blessed."

A Vision of Glory

My heart was burdened down by many a care,
I felt was more than I could longer bear;
To try to find a meaning for the tears,
Which seemed to be my meat so many years.

My Mother, sweetest, gentle, loving friend
Whose days had two years since come to an end,
Was waiting over on that golden shore
To welcome me, and I longed to cross o'er.

I'd laid my struggles out before my God
And talked to Him about the path I'd trod;
A path which seemed to always upward climb,
And asked Him for a strength that wasn't mine.

A sign that I was not alone while here,
To face the future which now seemed quite drear,
Was what I needed now to buoy me up
That I might have the strength to drink life's cup.

I turned to look towards my window, where
Above the kitchen sink, a flower fair,
Which Mom had nursed and babied 'till it grew
Now had long fronds and tiny blossoms, too.

The sun had moved across the heavens, so
It could not through my little window glow;
But there in that small corner of the room,
A light dispelled the shadows and the gloom.

A light I find it hard to now explain,
Came suddenly into my heart of pain;
And though it was so sudden and then gone,
The afterglow of that blest light goes on.

(Continued)

A Vision of Glory

(Continued)

I understood the message of the light
As clearly as if it had come by might,
And held me fast while speaking right out loud
"Fret not, for soon you'll go to be with God!"

A surge of joy welled up within me there,
I stared into that corner, and the care,
That I had felt now faded from my mind;
And all my troubles seemed to be behind.

I think an angel may have just been sent
To speak to me about the big event,
When I shall really, truly, fly away,
And enter that blest land of endless day.

No burdens and no tears will ever come,
To any who have gone to that glad home;
And no one who has gone would feign return —
It is the lovely land for which we yearn.

When trials and when burdens weigh us down,
And cause the heart to sigh and face to frown,
Remember, that each day we onward plod,
Brings us just one day closer to our God.

And He has promised perfect peace and rest
To all who live for Him and do their best
To please Him here and serve Him all the while.
And He is with us each and every mile.

"Lo, I am with you alway..."

The Valley

They say there is a valley dark
That I must walk some day;
And some folks seem to really dread it
So I have heard them say.
I read within the Shepherd's Psalm
About that valley dim;
That we shall have no fear of it
For we shall walk with Him,
Who walked the path that we must take
And knows it very well —
And after we've the valley crossed
With Him we'll always dwell.
Before I understood His love
I was afraid to "die"
Although I always thought I'd like
To live beyond the sky.
Without a valley we call "Death"
No heavenly home we'll see;
For that's the only way to life
With Christ eternally.
We have His love to comfort us
Through valleys here below;
And He has said He'll walk with us
Wherever we may go.
That means upon the mountain heights
Or in the vales below;
Whatever comes into our lives,
We know that this is so.
We know if He is with us, we
Will never need to fear;
The briars and thorns across the way —
He gently lifts them clear.

(Continued)

The Valley

(Continued)

The path we travel will be plain
As on our way we go,
Don't fear the valley, then, called "Death"
His promises are so.
We'll find the hand of Jesus reach
To lift our heavy load;
And He will go before us as
We walk life's weary road.
We never need to be afraid
When following after Him;
For in His light and in His love
There'll be no shadows dim.

Seven

Seven seems to be a magic number;
Think of all the things a boy can do —
When he's seven and is growing taller,
And stronger in his mighty muscles, too.
Now he rides a bike down past his neighbors
Where all the folks who know him wave and smile;
He spits out through a space where once a tooth grew,
And whistles as he stops to chat a while.
He's big enough to help his baby sister,
And strong enough to lift her up to look
At things he's making with his nails and hammer;
And smart enough to read to her a book.
He's definitely a helper for his Mother
And helps his Father work on cars and such,
But when it comes to doing chores assigned him,
He really doesn't cotton to that much.
He loves his Grandmas and his aunts and uncles,
And likes to visit with them when he can;
We hope he still comes often for those visits
When he has grown to be a great big man.
Six was such a nice age to remember,
But now I think this boy's in seventh heaven —
For when I ask, "How old are you this birthday?"
He squares his shoulders, grins, and says, "I'm seven!"

Just a Test

The taxes for my home had fallen due,
My car soon needed state inspection too;
The gas gauge on my car read "very low"
The rent was due another week or so.
My check this time, for which I'd given thanks
Was being divvied up between the banks;
The shelves whereon I stored my food were bare
With hardly any food I could prepare.
Inside my purse I had eleven cents
And there was not another source from whence
I could supply the things I needed now
And I just asked the Lord to show me how.
I turned my radio on then and the sound
I heard disturbed me and I quickly frowned;
And then a voice spoke out I'd heard before
When I had heard this siren's scary roar
"Don't be afraid, as this is just a test,
To make sure our equipment is the best."
I took that thought to heart and looked around
At all the things that caused my heart to pound
With worry over what might lie ahead;
And all this worry filled my heart with dread.
And then I thought I heard another voice
That made my heart with happiness rejoice
"Don't be afraid, as this is just a test
To see if you can trust Me for what's best."
And then, He said, "I've never let you down
So why is your brow wrinkled in that frown?
You know how well I clothe the lily fair
And watch the little birds up in the air
Can you then think I would forget to see
A child of mine whose needs apparent be?"

(Continued)

Just a Test

(Continued)
I recognized the voice and said, "Dear Lord,
Forgive me for not trusting in Your word;
I oftentimes forget when burdens press
That I can come to you in my distress."
My needs we then planned how we could obtain
And soon my problems were resolved again.
When you are "down" and with great burdens pressed
Remember, friend, that this is just a test.

What time I am afraid I will trust in Thee.

How Much I Owe

I have a lot of creditors,
to whom I am in debt;
It seems sometimes I owe much more
than I can ever pay;
But for the greatest debt I owe,
a bill I've never got —
For there is just no way that this debt
I can e'er repay.
You see, my life was full of sin,
and I could never give,
The price that was required to take
the debt for sin away;
A sacrifice was needed
that was pure and undefiled —
Whose blood could cleanse my heart
and for my awful sins then pay.
And so God sent His only Son
to die upon a cross;
He willingly laid down His life,
to take on Him my guilt.
He cleansed my soul, and washed it free
from all my sins and dross,
As for mankind, His Father,
through His death an altar built.
An altar where not only I,
but everyone on earth;
Can find release and pardon from
the debt to Him we owe;
And anyone who will may come
to Him for sweet release —
Then joyously go on his way
to serve God here below.

(Continued)

How Much I Owe

(Continued)
Commissioned then are we
who owe this debt of love to God;
To bear the news to others
that they may this freedom seek.
That for all troubled hearts,
our God will give His peace and love,
To all those calling on His name,
the lowly and the meek.
And when I think of what I owe
that I can never pay;
I thank and praise Him that He's taken
all my guilt and shame;
I have no "bill" for services
from God, though this is true;
My life and love to Him I give,
to ever praise His name.

October

October arrived quite late last night,
To stay a month, then go her way;
How beautiful her touch to earth,
How very brief will seem her stay.

Bright pumpkins piled in heaps of gold,
Corn fields with stubble brown of hue;
Apples and cider and turning leaves,
Show Harvest's signs in bold review.

Crisp, fragrant air, that quickens the gait
Pungent wood-smoke from campfires aglow;
Cause hearts to be thankful for blessings received,
Lovely October, these gifts doth bestow.

The Whistle

When I was just a little girl,
I used to watch my brother,
Put his hands together,
one on top the other;
And then he deftly blew upon
his hands a certain way.
And the noisy whistle that created
was heard a mile away.
I thought it would be lots of fun
to whistle like he did,
And he laughed at me and said that I
was just a little kid.
I didn't hold my hands right
and I never would learn how;
But I kept right on practicing,
and tried it anyhow.
I forgot about it as I grew,
and guess I just gave up
Because it seemed that I could never
learn my hands to cup.
Then one day, very suddenly,
when I was fifty-five,
I thought about that old time wish,
and gracious sakes alive,
I cupped my hands, and poised my thumbs,
and blew as best I could
And out came a better whistle
than I'd ever imagined would.
It took me fifty-five long years,
and yet I have no teeth
But that accomplishment made me smile
that I had got my wish.

(Continued)

The Whistle

(Continued)

Now if there's something you can't do,
that you've a mind to try
Don't give it up,
'cause you will probably do it by and by.
It doesn't need to be a wish
to whistle like my brother,
But it could be a lot of other things
that you would "druther"
So persevere, and you will find
that some day with surprise,
You'll do the thing you've wanted to
since the day you've been alive.
I just can't wait to tell my grandson
what I've learned to do
I don't believe I'll tell my kids,
you know they laugh at you
When you've grown slightly older
and still act like a kid;
But my grandson will probably practice
and be very glad *I* did.

My Treasures

My treasures are not made of silver or gold
Or diamonds or rubies or pearls;
But the things that are precious to me today
Are memories of three little girls —
And one little boy with eyes so blue
And freckles on his little face —
Four children so dear who brought joy to my heart
Leaving memories that time can't erase.

And treasures are pictures I saved in some books
To look at when I am alone;
Recalling with joy the times that we shared
Before from my care they were gone.
And memories are tender and sometimes bring tears,
That now they have drifted away;
So quickly and silently they each have gone
But in memory they're still here today.

I would not imprison them just so that I
Could have them with me every day;
For they are all near, and I surely take pride
In what they are doing today;
But in memory's garden I still can abide
And think of the days that we had
The joys that I knew with three little girls
And one little, dear little lad.

I've treasures anew, in the here and now
With another daughter so fine
Who has given to me and that son of mine
Two children with blue eyes that shine.
And two more fine sons have entered the clan
Bringing joy to my daughters and me
And there's still one daughter so dear to my heart
And as lovely as lovely can be.

(Continued)

My Treasures

(Continued)

No I would not wish that I could go back
And have them all babies again;
For then I would not have the memories sweet
Of all of the joys they have given.
But memory plays an important part
As I travel my pathway each day;
My treasures are not of silver or gold —
But I've wealth that will not pass away.

I'm writing of some of the treasures I have
That some day when homeward I've gone
To receive other treasures I've earned while here
My treasures can still linger on;
And I would tell each of my children that I
Still love each one of them the best —
And part of the mystery of this is that —
No one is loved more than the rest.

The Spider's Web

One day this week I looked out of a window,
High up inside the building where I work;
A big brown spider labored in a corner,
Wrapping insects; but his web would jerk,
As Fall winds whipped around where he was busy,
And often to a refuge he would run —
But always would return as it grew calmer
To finish up the work that he'd begun.
And then last night the sky grew dark and threatening;
And sometime during all that wild rainstorm,
The web, the insects and the big brown spider
Were washed away, and all his labors gone.
And when I went today to watch his progress
I felt a sense of grief that it should be
That everything for which he'd spent long hours
Was very suddenly gone, and so was he.
Sometimes when we have labored long and hard
For things that too can vanish overnight,
It seems to be a hard and cruel fate,
That sweeps away belongings from our sight;
But there are things that circumstances cannot
By buffeting, remove from out the heart;
And these are things eternal, far more precious
Than those material things from which we part.
Our memories, of other days we've treasured
Are ours from now until our lives are past;
And when some unexpected loss befalls us,
We still have treasures that will always last:
A faith to hold us when life's billows threaten
Our earthly treasures to dissolve away
A Father dear, to hear us when we whisper,
And answer every prayer that we may pray.

(Continued)

The Spider's Web

(Continued)

And we can know His love when we are burdened
By problems that we cannot understand;
No tempest can withdraw the calm assurance
We feel when we are safe within His hand.
Unlike the spider, which, when life is over,
Is dead, and nevermore has life and breath;
We triumph over problems that beset us
And conquer even in the face of death.
Though oftentimes we weave our webs of sorrow,
And in our weaving choose unwisely too,
The Master Weaver sees our faltering efforts
And steers us right if we to Him are true;
The spider's web reminds me as I labor
To trust not in the riches I might own
But ever by the Master Weaver's pattern,
To weave my treasures for my Heavenly home.

Do I Kiss Him
or Shake Hands?

Dear Jason, you are coming
to the age when I don't know
If I should kiss you, or shake hands,
or simply say, "hello."
I love you, oh, so very much,
and we're so far apart —
If I could see you, I'm quite sure,
I'd hug you to my heart.
We've had some really happy hours,
when you would visit me;
So, precious as those times were then,
to me you'll always be
A special lad, a priceless gift,
from God's own hand above;
And you have made my life so rich,
and filled my heart with love.
So on this day, when you are eight,
and a second-grader, too —
I send your card, and this small poem,
to say that I LOVE YOU.

If Winter Come —

(can Spring be far behind?)

Autumn passed so quietly I hardly had the time
To take much notice of her, as a hill I had to climb;
For I've been traveling hard along a path that I must take
Toward my destination, which I know that I must make
When Winter's gone away.

Quite suddenly I realized that Winter's really come;
Silver crowns my brow as I am on my journey home.
It seems the pace is quickening, I feel a sense of joy —
The kind I felt as in the Spring I'd found a brand new toy —
And then went traveling on.

Sweet Summer, how expectantly I waited for *her* call!
And now, in golden memory her blessings I recall;
The children which in love, my Father lent me for a while
In mem'ry still live in my heart and give me cause to smile —
As still I journey on.

And Autumn, hard upon the heels of Summer bright and gay
Was here with little warning, and I knew then that she'd stay
For only such a little while; I'd hoped that she'd be here
A longer time, but soon I felt a chill was in the air —
And Winter had her way.

Soon Winter too, will pass and I must say I'm rather glad —
She hasn't been exactly kind, and I am sometimes sad
For things that could be different,
which I've not power to change;
But I have no desire to try my life to rearrange
While Winter's here.

I'm busy now preparing, for I know that Spring will come;
Before I realize it's time, my journey will be done.

(Continued)

If Winter Come —

(Continued)

I'll climb that last long hill and I will say my last good-bye
And loved ones I have missed
will welcome me beyond the sky —
When Spring has come again.

Say, feel that warm and gentle breeze;
and what's that sweet refrain
That's coming to me from beyond that ridge
I'm trying to gain?
Oh, look! Can you believe such beauty really can exist?
In all my wildest dreams I never could have pictured this!
Say what? I'm HOME?

Index